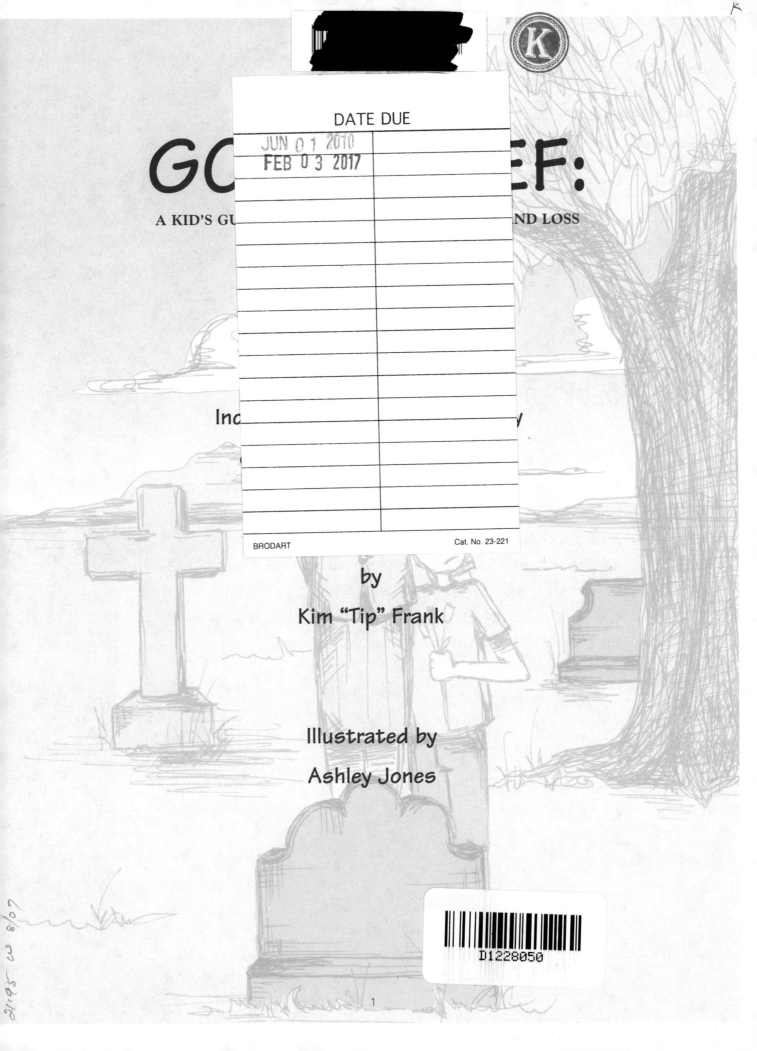

GO EF:

A KID'S GU ND LOSS

Inc y

by

Kim "Tip" Frank

Illustrated by

Ashley Jones

DEDICATION

This book is dedicated to my loving parents, Robert and Roberta Frank, who died many years ago. My parents left me a rich heritage. As caring parents and successful educators, my parents profoundly influenced me. Most of all, they taught me the values of getting a good education and the importance of caring about people. I am truly thankful to my mother and father. My parents' influence lives on!

A SPECIAL THANKS

Many thanks go to Bob and Susan Bowman for their special input involving this book. Bob and Susan spent countless moments encouraging me and offering many creative ideas throughout the process of publishing this book. I am greatly indebted to them for their professional input in my life and most of all for their friendship.

WHY THIS BOOK IS NEEDED

It has long been said that two constants in life are taxes and death. Even children cannot avoid the topic of death. It eventually affects us all, sometimes at very young ages. I have noticed in my roles as parent and counselor that healthy discussion about grief and loss greatly speeds up the healing process. Good Grief is designed to stimulate discussion around many of the issues that grief and loss create. As young people face the loss of a loved one and express their feelings and thoughts, the journey through grief occurs. Good Grief is a tool to help accomplish this purpose.

HOW TO UTILIZE THIS BOOK

This book can be used for small group counseling or just read individually. The book <u>Good Grief</u> was written to help youngsters in their journey through grief after the loss of a loved one. Children in upper elementary through middle school (grades 2-6) are the target audience. This book is self-paced. One can move along as fast or as slowly as desired. The main goal is to help youngsters think and talk about their experiences and feelings. By doing this, the healing process begins to take hold.

This book includes two separate booklets that can be reproduced and read with kids. The first booklet, Good Grief: Understanding Grief and Change, explains the grieving process in a conversational, matter-of-fact fashion. This section contains two or three thought-provoking questions after each page of the story. Because of time constraints in group settings, the group leader can choose which question(s) may be most appropriate for the group.

The second booklet involves the fictitious story, William's Great Loss. The story follows a child's experiences through the grieving process. Discussion questions are found throughout this section of the book as well.

Optional small group activities are included in the back of the book. These activities, which are divided into seven sessions, can be used at the discretion of the group leader before or after reading the book. Another option is to do these small group activities as lead-ins before reading different portions of the book.

THE FOCUS OF THE BOOK

The five common "stages of grief" are a special focus in this book. This "stage theory," first coined by Elizabeth Kubler-Ross in 1969, provides a backdrop for normal stages that children may experience around a loved one's death. The five steps or stages of grief that many people experience include:

- denial
- anger
- bargaining
- depression
- acceptance

These five (not necessarily sequential) stages are clearly seen in the reproducible story within this book called *William's Great Loss*. The goal is to help children see that these feelings and behaviors are normal and that there is hope that life will get better again in time.

The only way out of grief is to go through it. It is my hope that Good Grief will, in a very practical way, aid in the journey of finding hope and healing. Best wishes as this book is put to use!

Kim "Tip" Frank

WHAT WE KNOW ABOUT CHANGE AND LOSS IN CHILDREN

The way children respond to loss and change varies significantly. The following, however, are normal common responses to grief in children and adolescents. Keep in mind that the particular focus of this book involves children, preadolescents, and young teenagers.

COMMON WAYS KIDS RESPOND TO GRIEF

- Denial
- Anger
- Sadness
- Fear:
    - of abandonment
    - of parent(s) or other relatives dying
    - that they will *die*
    - of sickness (doctors, hospitals, etc.)
- Complaints of stomachaches/headaches, etc.
- Sleep problems such as insomnia and nightmares
- Loss of appetite
- Problems concentrating and sustaining tasks
- Withdrawal from friends and daily activities
- Regression (reverting to younger behaviors—"baby talking," thumb sucking, etc.)
- Hyperactivity ("wide open," boisterous play)
- Guilt:
    - From feeling they caused or should have prevented the death from occurring
    - From having fun while others are grieving
- Yearning for the loved one who died
- Difficulty talking about the deceased
- Drop in school performance
- Excessive questioning about or imitating the one who died
- Making statements about wanting to be with the deceased

SUGGESTIONS FOR PARENTS AND OTHER CAREGIVERS

As you can readily see, the ways kids grieve vary greatly. What is most important from a parent's or professional's standpoint is to monitor children's progress through the grief process. While these grief responses are normal and common, it is a <u>matter of degree</u> that must be noted.

There are three ways to measure if a problem is present or not. They are <u>intensity</u>, <u>frequency</u>, and <u>duration</u>. When grief responses persist and have more than normal intensity and frequency, it is wise to seek out professional help.

Family doctors and pediatricians can make referrals to a mental health professional such as a counselor, psychologist, or psychiatrist. Mental health professionals can provide a safe environment where children can talk about their feelings and gain valuable perspectives on death and dying. Mental health practitioners also consult with parents or guardians on how to help their child.

MORE WAYS PARENTS AND CAREGIVERS CAN HELP

Aside from monitoring your child's progress through the grief process and getting him/her professional help if necessary, there are many practical things you may do that are very simple. The following is a list of important and helpful strategies caring adults can provide to support their child.

- Don't be afraid to talk to your child about what happened. Kids take their leads from adults. If adults can face and talk about grief, kids will likely learn to talk through the grief process as well.

- Take time to really listen. Give your child your undivided attention when he or she wants to share thoughts and feelings.

- Maintain a normal routine. Kids feel more secure when life has a normal rhythm.

- Be honest with your child. Give him/her the facts about what has happened and about upcoming events without overburdening him/her with too much information. Keep it simple and straightforward.

- Tell him/her about what you know without exaggerating or minimizing the situation.

- Don't assume your child is too young to know what is happening.

- Provide more comfort and reassurance.

- Discuss what death is and what it means.

- Share personal experiences about losing special people in life. Help your child to see that you all will get through this time.

- Emphasize hope and courage.

- Encourage your child to creatively express feelings through writing, art, puppets, sand tray play, small group counseling, etc.

GOOD GRIEF:

Understanding Loss and Change

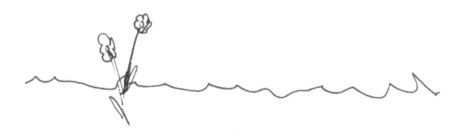

The famous cartoon character Charlie Brown often said, "Good grief!" when things didn't go his way. Good grief is exactly what we need when someone special in our lives dies.

DISCUSSION GUIDE

<u>Life will be different</u>

When someone special dies in our lives, we are greatly affected. Things change and are never the same again.

1. How has losing someone special changed your life?

2. Since life will be different now, what will you miss the most about the way it was?

Grief is the process a person goes through when a special person or thing such as a pet is lost in his or her life.

DISCUSSION GUIDE

<u>Grief brings feelings</u>

Grief involves the feelings we have when we have a change or loss in our lives. Sadness, worry, anger, and feeling upset are just a few emotions that people experience.

1. What feelings do you have about your loss?

2. Who is the person (or pet) in your life who has died?

We all experience grief when loss occurs. Since grief is going to happen in everyone's life at one time or another, we might as well make it "good grief."

DISCUSSION GUIDE

Everyone faces grief

It's good to know that you are not alone. Like you are doing now, everyone will have to face changes and losses sooner or later. This is a difficult but normal part of life.

1. Do you know someone else who has had to face a situation where someone has died? If so, who is it, and who did he or she lose?

2. What other kinds of losses and changes do people face? Have you personally experienced other kinds of losses or changes such as a parent's divorce, moving, etc.?

Good grief often involves working through five stages of grief. The main goal is to find a way to move on with life and find peace and hope.

DISCUSSION GUIDE

Keep your hope and courage alive

Yes, it is good to know that people do feel better in time. Over time life gets back to feeling normal again. It's different, but it can be okay. It is important to take two things with you as you go through the stages of grief. These are hope and courage.

1. What is your hope? How do you think life can be "okay" again someday? Where is your hope when someone dies?

2. How can you be strong and brave even in the loss of your loved one?

There are five steps or stages of grief that many people experience. They are as follows:

1) **Denial:** Acting like the loss or change never happened.

2) **Anger:** Feeling mad that this loss had to happen.

3) **Bargaining:** Wishful thinking that if you do certain good things, your loved one or pet will somehow come back and that life will be the same again.

4) **Depression:** Deep sadness about the loss, and not caring about normal things.

5) **Acceptance:** Taking what happened and finding peace about it.

DISCUSSION GUIDE

Grief takes time

Going through these stages takes time. Everyone grieves in his or her own way. It could be a short or long time before that "okay" feeling comes back.

1. How long have you been feeling grief?

2. Do you have hope that it will get better? Why or why not?

It is important to understand that a person like yourself doesn't always go through these stages in one, two, three order. In fact, many people experience all of these stages at different times.

DISCUSSION GUIDE

All feelings are O.K.

People grieve in different ways. There is no one way to go through the grieving process. There are, however, certain feelings and thoughts that most people experience. Thus, thoughts and feelings such as denial, anger and sadness are normal.

1. Are there one or two thoughts or feelings that you have often had?

2. What has the grieving process been like for you? Do you feel stuck on a certain stage, or do you feel like you are moving through the stages O.K.? Explain your answer.

You may go back and forth between the five stages as you experience grief. However, this process tends to move from stage one (denial) all the way through to eventually stage five (acceptance).

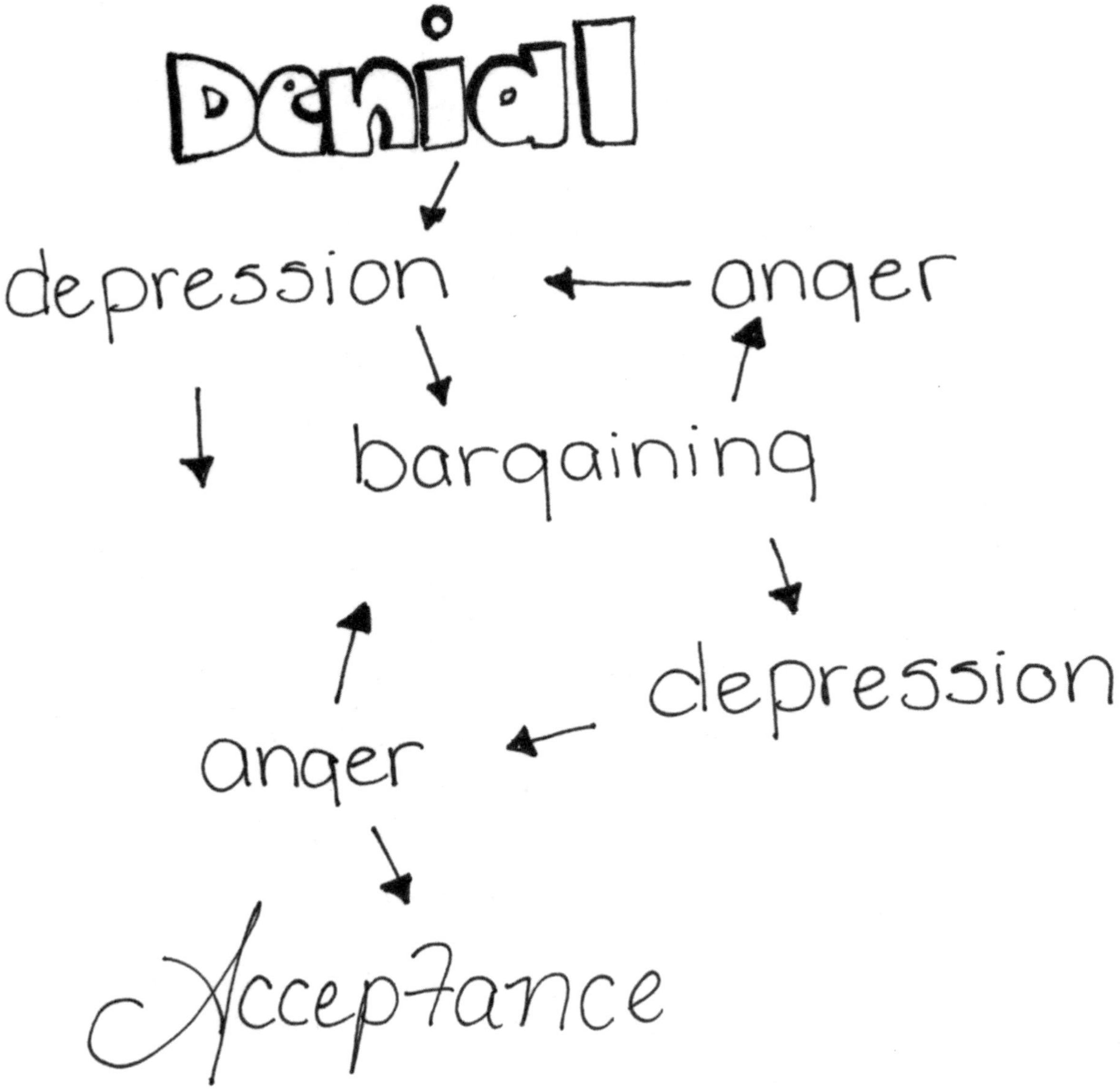

Denial

depression ← anger

↓ → bargaining ↗

anger ↗ ← depression

↘

Acceptance

DISCUSSION GUIDE

Grief has ups and downs

Here is where hope comes in. You'll get there! Things can and will get better. There will be ups and downs in the meantime. Hang in there!

1. Which, if any, of these stages fits your situation now?

❏ Denial

❏ Anger

❏ Bargaining

❏ Depression

❏ Acceptance

2. Do you feel like you have been moving back and forth between the five stages as you have experienced grief? If so, what stages are involved?

Everyone goes through grief at a different pace.
Weeks and sometimes months are needed to heal
from the loss of a loved one.

DISCUSSION GUIDE

Be good to yourself

A broken heart takes time to heal. Be patient and good to yourself as you go through this process. Again, keep your hope and courage alive.

1. What are some ways that you can be good to yourself?

2. What activities and people help bring joy into your life?

3. What has your pace been like in moving through grief? Would you rate it slow, medium, or fast? Explain your answer.

The following is the story of William, who is dealing with the loss of his grandfather. As you read the story, notice how he goes through the stages of grief.

DISCUSSION GUIDE

The closer we are, the stronger the feelings

William's story shows how someone might handle grief in his or her life. Notice how William struggles with the loss of his grandfather. The closer we feel toward the person who has died, the stronger the feelings of grief.

1. Describe your relationship with the person who died. How close were you to this person?

2. We can learn how to deal with a loss from others. Have you noticed how others have dealt with someone special dying? If so, what have you learned from them?

WILLIAM'S GREAT LOSS

BY TIP FRANK

William was ten years old when he got the news about his grandfather. Grandpa Joe died after a long illness. William thought it would never happen, but it did.

DISCUSSION GUIDE

Sometimes when people die it happens suddenly and unexpectedly. In William's case, his grandfather was sick for a long time. William thought somehow that his grandfather would recover.

1. In your situation did it happen suddenly, or could you see things slowly getting worse?

2. Did you have hope that your loved one would somehow recover? Explain your answer.

Denial

Upon hearing the bad news from his mother, William sat and said no words. He didn't even cry. He thought surely this could not be happening. Even at the funeral, William just sat and talked very little.

DISCUSSION GUIDE

William was in shock. To protect himself from the hurt of losing his grandfather, William blocked most of it out of his mind as if it never happened.

1. Did you find yourself pushing your feelings aside or pretending that it didn't happen?

2. Why do you think people block unhappy thoughts and feelings out of their minds?

For several weeks William acted like nothing happened. He just went to school and did his homework. William played with the other kids, but the one thing he didn't do was talk about his grandfather.

DISCUSSION GUIDE

William thought by pushing his feelings away and not dealing with them that life could somehow be normal. He just stayed on his normal routine as if nothing happened.

1. How did you handle getting the bad news about the loss of your loved one?

2. How did you act and feel in the following days and weeks?

Anger

In the weeks that followed, the reality of not seeing his grandfather set in. William felt the loss of his grandfather greatly. Grandpa Joe was no longer around to take him to the store and buy him a candy bar like he always did. Grandpa was not there to go fishing with him and give him good advice.

DISCUSSION GUIDE

William could not bring his grandfather back, nor can you bring your loved one back. However, we don't have to lose the memories we have of the one who has died. We can keep good memories in our hearts for a lifetime.

1. What memories do you want to treasure in your mind?

2. Is there any special advice or any particular thing that you learned from the one who has died?

3. How would you rate your anger following the loss of your loved one?

William grew more and more angry and frustrated about his loss. He started arguing with his parents, which William had never done before. William even got into a fight with his best friend. William seemed mad at the world. How unfair it seemed not to have his special grandpa around him.

DISCUSSION GUIDE

It is okay to be angry. Everyone gets angry at one time or another. However, it is important to move past it as soon as possible. Acting out angry feelings or holding them inside only makes matters worse. It is a good idea to have a "chill out plan." Having two or three things you can do to overcome angry feelings helps. Exercise, friends, and good activities can bring relief.

1. What can you do when you feel mad? (Caution: Make sure that it is not against the rules or laws and that it won't hurt you or others.)

2. While it is O.K. to be angry, what are some healthy rules about anger? (Emphasize: You can't hurt yourself; you can't hurt others; and you can't hurt property.)

Bargaining

William wished somehow, someway Grandpa Joe could be back. William thought maybe, just maybe, if he were good enough, Grandpa would come back. William promised himself that he would follow the rules, do his chores, and work hard to get good grades at school.

DISCUSSION GUIDE

William thought that somehow he could change things by being good enough. The truth is that he could not bring his grandfather back anymore than you could bring back your loved one. It is, however, normal to wish you could make it happen.

1. Have you tried to wish or bargain your loved one back? If so, how have you tried to do this?

2. While you cannot change the fact that someone died, you can control a lot of things in your life. What things can you personally control? Grades, friendships, and involvement in activities are some good examples.

William worked hard and prayed that Grandpa Joe would return into his life. Over time, though, William realized this wasn't happening. Grandpa Joe was gone and would not be returning.

DISCUSSION GUIDE

The truth was hard for William to take. All his efforts did not work. A good way to understand this is by knowing the 3 C's of grief.

The Three C's

1. I didn't cause it.

2. I can't change it.

3. I can cope.

Coping means that you can work through it in the best way possible. Coping, also, means finding a way to go on with your life. Remind yourself that you can make it through this time. Perhaps you will want to write down the three C's of grief and memorize them.

1. Did you somehow feel that you were responsible for the loss of your loved one? If so, in what

way? (Emphasize that guilt is a normal feeling to have when someone dies; however, the death is not your fault.)

2. How well are you coping with your loss? Rate yourself on a scale of 1-3.

    1 = I'm having difficulty.

    2= I'm doing O.K.

    3= I'm coping well.

Depression

William didn't seem to care about anything once he realized that Grandpa Joe was gone. He no longer played with his friends or watched his favorite team play football. William picked at his food and quit doing much of his schoolwork. Even though his teacher and mother fussed at William for not doing his work and not taking care of himself, it didn't matter to William. Until . . .

DISCUSSION GUIDE

William felt *deep* sadness. He lost interest in most everything, even in things he normally loved to do. He quit caring about hanging out with his friends and taking care of himself. William had a hard time accepting the fact that he couldn't change what happened.

While it is normal to have blue (sad) feelings when someone dies, it is very important not to get stuck on these feelings. If sad feelings last, seeing a counselor or doctor can help. Somehow talking to someone who cares helps sad feelings to lift away.

1. Have you had long-lasting sadness? If so, how have these feelings affected you?

2. Who are the people with whom you can talk about your feelings and problems?

Acceptance

Time went by and William went to see an understanding counselor. The counselor explained that his feelings were normal and that sooner or later his broken heart would heal.

DISCUSSION GUIDE

The sun eventually shines after times of clouds and rain. Sometimes the feelings of grief hang around, but eventually a peace inside shines through.

1. Have you found any peace inside of you yet?

2. How do counselors help people's hearts to heal?

The counselor even shared a secret code that helped speed up the grieving process.

The secret code is:

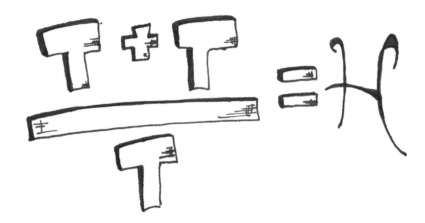

DISCUSSION GUIDE

A broken heart can take a long time to heal. Remembering this secret code, which is explained on the next page, can help greatly. You may want to write this secret code on a card and keep it handy.

1. What secrets have you learned for making it through tough times?

2. What do you think the secret code stands for?

The secret code:

The secret code stands for:

DISCUSSION GUIDE

As mentioned earlier, talking about your feelings with people who care about you is sure to help. Giving yourself permission to cry is wise. Tears let our feelings out.

Share the secret code with someone else. It may encourage them. As you reach out and help others, you will feel better and better.

1. With whom could you share the secret code?

2. How often do you share your real feelings with people you trust?

3. Do you feel free to cry when you have sad or upset feelings? Why or why not?

As William talked about his feelings, he began to feel better and better. He even learned that it was okay to cry when he felt like it. As William talked and let out his tears, his broken heart did start to heal. Eventually, in fact, life got back to normal for the most part.

DISCUSSION GUIDE

One day William realized that he was feeling better. Life felt good again. He was going on with his life. Friends, good grades, and normal activities were all a part of his life again. How good it felt to be alive and well!

1. What are some ways you will know that life is getting back to normal for you?

2. What was life like before the death of your loved one? Do you think you can get back to a normal life again? Explain your answer.

Oh, those sad feelings come back from time to time for William. He still gets mad sometimes. William often wishes his Grandpa Joe could still do things with him. But . . .

DISCUSSION GUIDE

You may experience feelings of grief from time to time because your loved one was a special part of your life. Holidays, places, events, and other things will often remind you of this person. And while feelings will come back at times, there is still a certain peace that will make life seem okay.

1. What situations or things remind you of the loved one that you miss?

2. What can you do to feel better again when unpleasant feelings come back?

William knows he has those good memories and the great lessons he learned from his grandfather in his heart. He'll never forget Grandpa Joe, and William knows that his Grandpa Joe would want him to go on with his life.

DISCUSSION GUIDE

Going on with your life does not mean forgetting the one who died. You can keep him or her in your heart. There is no need for guilty feelings as you get on with life.

You may want to have a special keepsake to remind you of the one you have in your heart. A favorite picture, present, or object that has special meaning would be a good way to keep positive feelings and memories alive.

1. What keepsake or special item could you find to keep the one who has died in your heart?

2. What is your best memory of your loved one who died?

So, he will go on with living his life to the fullest! And, William will make his grandpa proud!

DISCUSSION GUIDE

As William did, you can go on to do great things in your life.

1. What would be some good goals for you to try to accomplish?

2. How could you make people proud of you?

The End.

OPTIONAL SMALL GROUP ACTIVITIES

The activities in the following seven sessions can be used in various ways. They can serve as introductory activities to prepare students for the book or as culminating activities after reading the story. These activities may best be used while reading the story. They can be utilized as "lead-ins" when different portions of the book are read.

SESSION ONE: MEET AND GREET

Icebreaker

Using a roll of toilet paper, have each student pull off any number of squares (suggest between 1 and 7). For each square taken, each student states one fact about themselves that they don't mind sharing (i.e., favorite hobby, food, subject in school, place visited, etc.).

Group Rules

Discuss the three group rules.

1) Look at the person who is talking.

2) Be nice to yourself and others.

3) What we say in here stays in here. (Note this involves the personal things that group members share. The main points taught in lessons can be shared with parents, friends, etc. Carefully discuss the meaning of confidentiality.)

Activity

Have each person who would like to share tell about the person (or pet) they have lost.

SESSION TWO: GRIEF SCULPTURE

Icebreaker

Have group members share their highlight of the last week (i.e., a good grade on a test, a fun time with a friend, etc.).

Activity

Using clay or modeling dough, have each group member make an object that describes how he or she feels about the loss of his or her loved one.

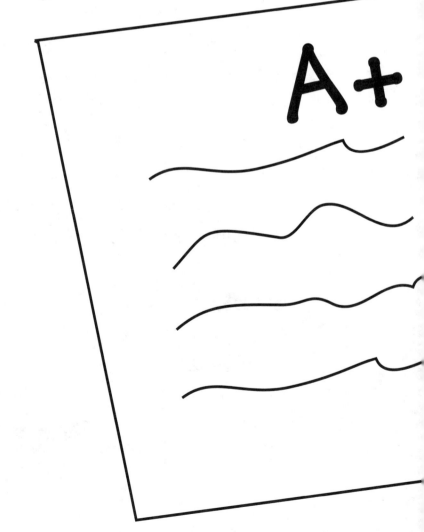

SESSION THREE: FRAMING GRIEF

Icebreaker

Have each member of the group find a common object in the room (a ball, marker, piece of chalk, eraser, book, etc.) that describes him or her. Each person can then explain how it relates to him or her.

Activity

Ask each person to draw a picture using the following reproducible page of what death means to him or her. Have each person talk about his or her drawing.

Draw your feelings about what
death or dying means to you.

SESSION FOUR: RASing FEELINGS

Icebreaker

Using the following reproducible page, have group members attempt to unscramble the secret code word called **RAS**. See how many students can unscramble the words within two minutes.

Activity One

Discuss the secret code word. Explain that this is a formula for what to do with feelings.

    R stands for **Recognize your feelings**

    A stands for **Accept your feelings**

    S stands for **Share your feelings**

Activity Two

See which student can come up with the most feeling words related to grief using the accompanying page called "Feeling Word Race." Set a time limit of ninety seconds. Then make a compilation of all the words the group generated.

Activity One

RAS Your Feelings

Unscramble the secret code.

O G C Z R E E I N

_ _ _ _ _ _ _ _ _

C E C T P A

_ _ _ _ _ _

R E H S A

_ _ _ _ _

_____ , _____ , and
_____ your feelings.

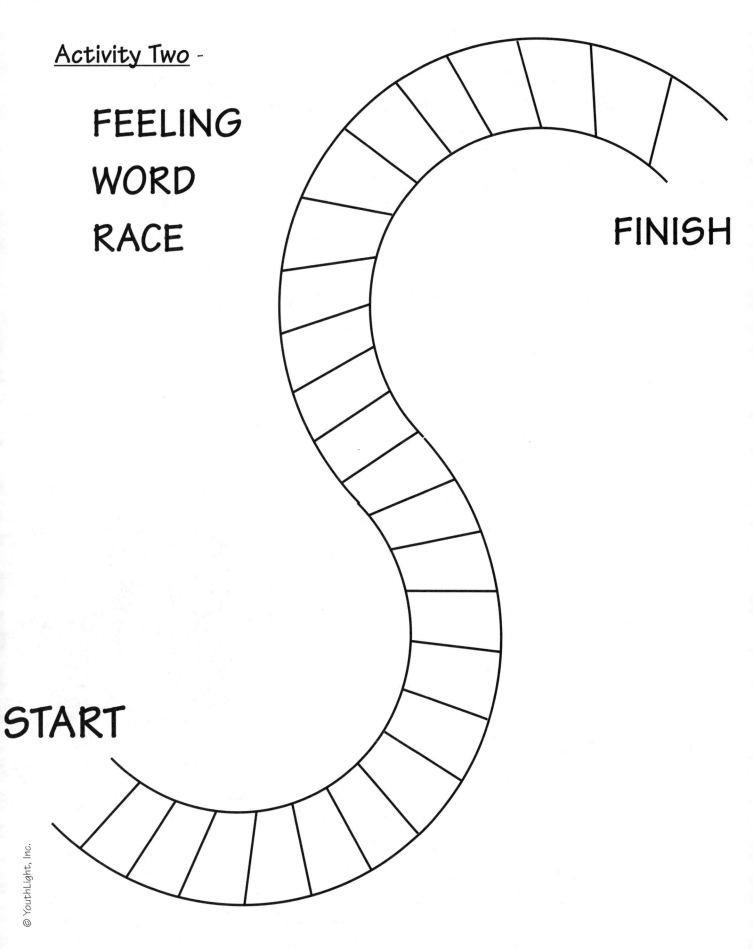

Activity Two -

FEELING
WORD
RACE

FINISH

START

SESSION FIVE: THE COPING CAN

Icebreaker

Using a foam ball, play a game of "hot potato." As each person catches the ball, he or she quickly needs to share a thought about how his or her life is going in a word or phrase before throwing the ball to someone else. Emphasize how life goes on even while people grieve.

Activity

The group leader prepares for the session by bringing in an empty soup can. Use the accompanying reproducible "label" on the next page. Cut out this label called "The Coping Can" and glue or tape it to the can. Now on a small scrap of paper, have each group member write down his or her best idea for coping or dealing with loss (i.e., exercise, talking to trusted adults and friends, playing a computer game, prayer, etc.). Have each person put his or her ideas in the can. The group leader then reads and discusses each idea with the group.

prayer

exercise

talking

THE COPING CAN

Cut and paste the
label on a soup can.

the *Coping Can*

SESSION SIX: MAKING LEMONADE

Icebreaker

Play a game of charades. Ask each group member to act out a feeling that he or she has had lately. The other members try to guess each feeling that is being acted out.

Activity

Show a lemon to the group. Talk about how one of the purposes of our group is to turn lemons into lemonade. Discuss how losing a loved one can be bittersweet like lemonade. While it is difficult to lose someone special, we can keep this person in our hearts. Ask the group members, "What is one of your best memories with this person?" Remind the group to treasure these memories.

Homework

Ask each person in the group to bring in a picture of the person who died or bring in an object that is a good reminder of this person.

Also, use the accompanying reproducible page called "My Treasured Memories." Have each

group member fill out the information and bring it back to the next session.

74

MY TREASURED MEMORIES

My treasured memories of _____

By _____ (your name)

Date _____

What _____ meant to me:

_____

_____

_____

_____

Best memories:

_____

_____

_____

_____

The most important thing I learned from_____:

_____

_____

_____

_____

SESSION SEVEN: TREASURED MEMORIES

Icebreaker

Do a trust bounce. Divide the group into pairs. (You may have to participate.) Using a small rubber ball, see which pair can bounce the ball back and forth the most times without missing it. Have each pair take a turn standing about ten to fifteen feet apart. Briefly discuss how the group has learned to cooperate, support, and trust each other.

Activity

Have each person share his or her picture or object along with the reproducible handout called "My Treasured Memories" (see homework from Session Six). Each group member is encouraged to celebrate his or her loved one's life by sharing what he or she meant to him or her.

Finally, provide a manila envelope for each student. On each envelope write "My Treasured Memories." Have each member keep any pictures, small objects, handouts from the group, etc. in the envelope as good remembrances of the person who has died. Explain that the contents in this manila envelope will one day be treasured memories of their loved ones. Encourage the group members to put this "My Treasured Memories" envelope in a special place for safekeeping.